PowerKiDS
Readers
SAFARI ANIMALS

LIONS

Clara Reade

PowerKiDS
press™
New York

For Anita Rose Buznitz Williams

Published in 2013 by The Rosen Publishing Group, Inc.
29 East 21st Street, New York, NY 10010

First Edition

Editor: Amelie von Zumbusch
Book Design: Greg Tucker

Photo Credits: Cover, pp. 5, 7, 9, 11, 13, 15, 17, 21, 23, 24 Shutterstock.com; p. 19 iStockphoto/Thinkstock.

Library of Congress Cataloging-in-Publication Data

Reade, Clara.
  Lions / by Clara Reade. — 1st ed.
      p. cm. — (Powerkids Readers: Safari animals)
  Includes index.
  ISBN 978-1-4488-7391-3 (library binding) — ISBN 978-1-4488-7470-5 (pbk.) —
ISBN 978-1-4488-7543-6 (6-pack)
  1. Lion—Juvenile literature. I. Title.
  QL737.C23R43 2013
  599.757—dc23
                                                2011043880

Manufactured in the United States of America

CPSIA Compliance Information: Batch #CS12PK: For Further Information contact Rosen Publishing, New York, New York at 1-800-237-9932

CONTENTS

Lions are big cats.

Big cats are cats that
can roar.

A group of lions is a **pride**.

8

9

Baby lions are **cubs**.

Male lions have **manes**.

13

Most lions live in Africa.

A few lions live in Asia.

Lions live in zoos, too.

18

Lions eat meat.

They team up to hunt.

23

WORDS TO KNOW

cubs

mane

pride

WEBSITES

Due to the changing nature of Interne links, PowerKids Press has developed an online list of websites related to the subject of this book. This site is update regularly. Please use this link to acces: the list:
www.powerkidslinks.com/pkrs/lions/